Wisdoms of the East

The Confessions of Al Ghazali

Translated By

Claud Field, M.A.

Qadeem Press

Qadeem Press

Qadeem Press Edition
Breathing Life into Forgotten Pages
www.qadeempress.com

Reprinted by Qadeem Press in 2025

Find our titles on your favourite online bookstore using the keyword 'Qadeem Press'

Contents

Editorial note

The object of the Editors of this series is a very definite one. They desire above all things that, in their humble way, these books shall be the ambassadors of good-will and understanding between East and West-the old world of Thought and the new of Action. In this endeavour, and in their own sphere, they are but followers of the highest example in the land. They are confident that a deeper know- ledge of the great ideals and lofty philosophy of Oriental thought may help to a revival of that true spirit of Charity which neither despises nor fears the notions of another creed and colour. Finally, in thanking press and public for the very cordial reception given to the "Wisdom of the East" Series, they wish to state that no pains have been spared to secure the best specialists for the treatment of the various subjects at hands.

L. Cranmer-Byng
S.A. Kapadia

Northbrook Society
185 Piccadilly, W

Introduction

Birth of Ghazali

ABOU HAMID MUHAMMAD IBN MUHAMMED AL GHAZZALI was born in the city of Tus in Khorassan, A.D. 1058, one year after the great poet and free thinker Abu'l Ala died. He was the son of a dealer in cotton thread (Ghazzal), whence his name. Losing his father in early life, he was confided to the care of a Sufi, whose influence extended through his subsequent career. On finishing his studies he was appointed professor of theology at Bagdad. Here he achieved such splendid success that all the Imams became his zealous partisans. So great, indeed, was his renown, so ardent the admiration he inspired, that the Muhammadans sometimes said: "If all the books of Islam were destroyed, it would be but a slight loss, provided Al Ghazali's work on the Revivification of the Sciences of Religion were preserved." The following short treatise gives the history of the mind of this remarkable man in his pursuit of truth. It might not inaptly bear the title "Confessions of an Inquiring Spirit." In its intellectual subtlety it bears a certain resemblance to Newman's Grammar of Assent, and in its almost Puritanical sense of the terrors of the world to come, it is akin to Bunyan's Grace Abounding. It is also interesting as being one of the very few specimens of genuine Eastern autobiography.

After describing the difficulty with which he escaped from an almost Pyrrhonic scepticism, "not by systematic reasoning and accumulation of proofs, but by a flash of light which God sent into my soul," he reviews the various sects whom he encountered in his search for truth:

I. The scholastic theologians, who profess to follow reason and speculation.

II. The philosophers, who call themselves masters of Logic and Demonstration.

III. The Sufis, who claim an immediate in- tuition, and who perceive the real manifestation of truth as common men perceive material phenomena.

After mastering the first two systems and still finding the great problem unsolved, he was forced to pronounce philosophy incompetent, and to seek in some higher faculty than reason the solution of his doubts. The intuition or ecstasy ("wajd") of the Sufis was to him a sort of revelation. His search for truth occupied several years, in the course of which he renounced his professorship of theology at Bagdad and went into devotional retirement at Jerusalem and Damascus, and also performed the pilgrimage to Mecca.

He returned for a short time to Nishapur, the birthplace of Omar Khayyam, his elder contemporary, whom, as Professor Browne tells us in his History of the Persian Literature, he met and disliked. He finally went back to Tus, his native place, where he died, A.D. 1111. Professor D B Macdonald, in an article on Ghazali in Journal of the American Oriental Society, quotes the following account of his death as related by his brother Ahmad, "On Monday at dawn my brother performed the ablutions and prayed. Then he said, 'Bring me my grave- clothes,' and he took them and kissed them, and laid them on his eyes and said, 'I hear and obey the command to go into the King'. And he stretched out his feet and went to meet Him and was taken to the good-will of God Most High."

The great service which Al-Ghazali rendered to the Sufis was, as Mr. Whinfield has pointed out, in the preface to his translation of the Masnavi, to provide them with a metaphysical terminology, which he had derived from the writings of Plotinus the Neo-Platonist. He also gave them a secure position in the Church of Islam.

In his Development of Muslim Theology, Professor Macdonald calls Ghazali "the greatest, certainly the most sympathetic figure in the history of Islam, and the only teacher of the after generations ever put by a Muslim on a level with the four great Imams" He further says of him: Islam has never outgrown him, has never fully understood him. In the renaissance of Islam which is now rising to view, his time will come, and the new life will proceed from a renewed study of his works."

The Confessions of Al Ghazali

Ghazali's search for truth

"In the name of the most merciful God"

QUOTH the Imam Ghazali:

Glory be to God, whose praise should precede every writing and every speech! May the blessings of God rest on Muhammed His Prophet and His Apostle, on his family and companions by whose guidance error is escaped!

You have asked me, O brother in the faith, to expound the aim and the mysteries of religious sciences, the boundaries and depths of theological doctrines. You wish to know my experiences while disentangling truth lost in the medley of sects and divergencies of thought, and how I have dared to climb from the low levels of traditional belief to the topmost summit of assurance. You desire to learn what I have borrowed, first of all, from scholastic theology; and secondly from the method of the Ta'limites, who, in seeking truth, rest upon the authority of a leader; and why, thirdly, I have been led to reject philosophic systems; and finally, what I have accepted of the doctrine of the Sufis, and the sum total of truth which I have gathered in studying every variety of opinion. You ask me why, after resigning at Bagdad a teaching post which attracted a number of hearers, I have, long afterwards, accepted a similar one at Nishapur. Convinced as I am of the sincerity which prompts your inquiries, I proceed to answer them, invoking the help and protection of God.

Know then, my brother (may God direct you in the right way), that the diversity in beliefs and religions, and the variety of doctrines and sects which divide men, are like a deep ocean strewn with shipwrecks, from which very few escape safe and sound. Each sect, it is true, believes itself in possession of the truth and of salvation, "each party," as the Koran saith, "rejoices in its own creed"; but as the Chief of the apostles, whose word is always truthful, has told us, "My people will be divided into more than seventy sects, of whom only one will be saved." This prediction, like all others of the Prophet, must be fulfilled.

From the period of adolescence, that is to say, previous to reaching my twentieth year to the present time when I have passed my fiftieth, I have ventured into this vast ocean; I have fearlessly sounded its depths, and like a resolute diver, I have penetrated its darkness and dared its dangers and abysses. I have interrogated the beliefs of each sect and scrutinised the mysteries of each doctrine, in order to disentangle truth from error and orthodoxy from heresy. I have never met one who maintained the hidden meaning of the Koran without investigating the nature of his belief, nor a partisan of its exterior sense without inquiring into the results of his doctrine. There is no philosopher whose system I have not fathomed, nor theologian the intricacies of whose doctrine I have not followed out.

Sufism has no secrets into which I have not penetrated; the devout adorer of Deity has revealed to me the aim of his austerities; the atheist has not been able to conceal from me the real reason of his unbelief. The thirst for knowledge was innate in me from an early age; it was like a second nature implanted by God, without any will on my part. No sooner had I emerged from boyhood than I had already broken the fetters of tradition and freed myself from hereditary beliefs.

Having noticed how easily the children of Christians become Christians, and the children of Moslems embrace Islam, and remembering also the traditional saying ascribed to the Prophet, "Every child has in him the germ of Islam, then his parents make him Jew, Christian, or Zoroastrian," I was moved by a keen desire to learn what was this innate disposition in the child, the nature of the accidental belief imposed on him by the authority of his parents and his masters, and finally the unreasoned convictions which he derives from their instructions.

Struck with the contradictions which I encountered in endeavouring to disentangle the truth and falsehood of these opinions, I was led to make the following reflection: "The search after truth being the aim which I propose to myself, I ought in the first place to ascertain what are the bases of certitude." In the next place I recognised that certitude is the clear and complete knowledge of things, such knowledge as leaves no room for doubt nor possibility of error and conjecture, so that there remains no room in the mind for error to find an entrance. In such a case it is necessary that the mind, fortified against all possibility of going astray, should embrace such a strong conviction that, if, for example, anyone possessing the power of changing a stone into gold, or a stick into a serpent, should seek to shake the bases of this certitude, it would remain firm and immovable. Suppose, for instance, a man should come and say to me, who am firmly convinced that ten is more than three, "No; on the contrary, there is more than ten, and, to prove it, I change this rod into a serpent," and supposing that he actually did so, I should remain none the less convinced of the falsity of his assertion, and although his miracle might arouse my astonishment, it would not instil any doubt into my belief.

I then understood that all forms of knowledge which do not unite these conditions (imperviousness to doubt, etc.) do not deserve any confidence, because they are not beyond the reach of doubt, and what is not impregnable to doubt cannot constitute certitude.

The Subterfuges of the Sophists

I then examined what knowledge I possessed, and discovered that in none of it, with the exception of sense-perceptions and necessary principles, did I enjoy that degree of certitude which I have just described. I then sadly reflected as follows: "We cannot hope to find truth except in matters which carry their evidence in themselves-that is to say, in sense-perceptions and necessary principles; we must therefore establish these on a firm basis. Is my absolute confidence in sense perceptions and on the infallibility of necessary principles analogous to the confidence which I formerly possessed in matters believed on the authority of others; Is it only analogous to the reliance most people place on their organs of vision, or is it rigorously true without admixture of illusion or doubt?"

I then set myself earnestly to examine the notions we drive from the evidence of the senses and from sight in order to see if they could be called in question. The result of a careful examination was that my confidence in them was shaken. Our sight for instance, perhaps the best practised of all our senses, observes a shadow, and finding it apparently stationary pronounces it devoid of movement. Observation and experience, however, show subsequently that a shadow moves not suddenly, it is true, but gradually and imperceptibly, so that it is never really motionless.

Again, the eye sees a star and believes it as large as a piece of gold, but mathematical calculations prove; on the contrary, that it is larger than the earth. These notions, and all others which the senses declare, true, are subsequently contradicted and convicted of falsity in an irrefragable manner by the verdict of reason.

Then I reflected in myself, "Since I cannot trust to the evidence of my senses, I must rely only on intellectual notions based on funda- mental principles, such as the following axioms: 'Then is more than three. Affirmation and negation cannot coexist together. A thing cannot both be created and also existent from eternity living and annihilated simultaneously, at once necessary and impossible." To this the notions

I derived from my senses made the following dejections: "Who can guarantee you that you can trust to the evidence of reason more than to that of the senses? You believed in our testimony till it was contradicted by the verdict of reason, otherwise you would have continued to believe it to this day. Well, perhaps, there is above reason another judge who, if he appeared, would convict reason of falsehood, just as reason has confuted us. And if such a third arbiter is not yet apparent, it does not follow that he does not exist."

To this argument, I remained some time without reply; a reflection drawn from the phenomena of sleep deepened my doubt. "Do you not see," I reflected, "that while asleep you assume your dreams to be indisputably real? Once awake, you recognise them for what they are- baseless chimeras. Who can assure you, then, of the reliability of notions which, when awake, you derive from the senses and from reason? In relation to your present state, they may be real; but it is possible also that you may enter upon another state of being which will bear the same relation to your present state as this does to your condition when asleep. In that new sphere you will recognise that the conclusion of reason are only chimeras."

This possible condition is perhaps, that which the Sufis call "ecstasy" ("hal"), that is to say, according to them, a state in which, absorbed in themselves and in the suspension of sense-perceptions, they have visions beyond the reach of intellect. Perhaps also Death is that state, according to that saying of the prince of prophets: "Men are asleep; when they die, they wake." Our present life in relation to the future is perhaps only a dream and man, once dead, will see things in direct opposition to those now before his eyes; he will then understand that word of the Koran, "To-day We have removed the veil from thine eyes and thy sight is keen."

Such thoughts as these threatened to shake my reason, and I sought to find an escape from them. But how? In order to disentangle the knot of this difficulty, a proof was necessary. Now a proof must be based on primary assumptions, and it was precisely these of which I was in doubt. This unhappy state lasted about two months, during which I was not, it is true, explicitly or by profession but morally and essentially a thorough-going sceptic.

God at last deigned to heal me of this mental malady; my mind recovered sanity and equilibrium, the primary assumptions of reason re- covered with me all their stringency and force. I owed my deliverance, not to a concatenation of proofs and arguments, but to the light which God caused to penetrate into my heart--the light which illuminates the threshold of all knowledge. To suppose that certitude can be only based upon formal arguments is to limit the boundless mercy of God. Someone asked the Prophet the explanation of this passage in the Divine Book: "God opens to Islam the heart of him whom He chooses to direct" That is spoken," replied the Prophet, "of the light which God sheds in the heart." "And how can man recognise that light?" he was asked. "By his detachment from this world of illusion and by a secret drawing towards the eternal world," the Prophet replied.

On another occasion he said: "God has created His creatures in darkness, and then has shed upon them His light." It is by the help of this light that the search for truth must be carried on. As by His mercy this light descends from time to time among men, we must ceaselessly be on the watch for it. This is also corroborated by another saying of the Apostle: "God sends upon you, at certain times, breathings of His grace; be prepared for them."

My object in this account is to make others understand with what earnestness we should search for truth, since it leads to results we never dreamt of. Primary assumptions have not got to be sought for, since they are always present to our minds; if we engage in such a search, we only find them persistently elude our grasp. But those who push their investigation beyond ordinary limits are safe from the suspicion of negligence in pursuing what is within their reach.

The different kinds of seekers after truth

Whren God in the abundance of His mercy had healed me of this malady, I ascertained that those who are engaged in the search for truth may be divided into three groups.

I. Scholastic theologians, who profess to follow theory and speculation.
II. The Philosophers, who profess to rely upon formal logic.
III. The Sufis, who call themselves the elect of God and possessors of intuition and knowledge of the truth by means of ecstasy.

"The truth," I said to myself, must be found among these three classes of men who devote themselves to the search for it. If it escapes them, one must give up all hope of attaining it. Having once surrendered blind belief, it is im- possible to return to it, for the essence of such belief is to be unconscious of itself. As soon as this unconsciousness ceases it is shattered like a glass whose fragments cannot be again reunited except by being cast again into the furnace and refashioned." Determined to follow these paths and to search out these systems to the bottom, I proceeded with my investigation in the following order: Scholastic theology; philosophical systems: and, finally Sufism.

The aim of Scholastic Theology and its results

Commencing with theological science, I care- fully studied and mediated upon it. I read the writings of the authorities in this department and myself composed several treatises. I recognised that this science, while sufficing its own requirements, could not assist me in arriving at the desired goal. In short, its object is to preserve the purity of orthodox beliefs from all heretical innovation. God, by means of His Apostle, has revealed to His creatures a belief which is true as regards their temporal and eternal interests; the chief articles of it are laid down in the Koran and in the traditions. Subsequently, Satan suggested to innovators principles contrary to those of orthodoxy; they listened greedily to his suggestions, and the purity of the faith was menaced God then raised up a school of theologians and inspired them with the desire to defend orthodoxy by means of a system of proofs adapted to unveil the devices of the heretics and to foil the attacks which they made on the doctrines established by tradition.

Such is the origin of 'scholastic theology, many of its adepts, worthy of their high calling valiantly defended the orthodox faith by proving the reality of prophecy and the falsity of heretical innovations. But, in order to do so, they had to rely upon a certain number of premises, which they accepted in common with their adversaries, and which authority and universal consent or simply the Koran and the traditions obliged them to accept. Their principal effort was to expose the self-contradictions of their opponents and to confute them by means of the premises which they had professed to accept. Now a method of argumentation like this has little value for one who only admits self-evident truths. Scholastic theology could not consequently satisfy me nor heal the malady from which I suffered.

It is true that in its later development theology was not content merely to defend dogma; it betook itself to the study of first principles of substances, accidents and the laws which govern them; but through want of a thoroughly scientific basis, it could not advance far in its researches, nor succeed in dispelling entirely the overhanging obscurity which spring from diversities of belief.

I do not, however, deny that it has had a more satisfactory result for others; on the contrary, I admit that it has; but it is by introducing the principles of authority in matters which are not self-evident. Moreover. my object is to explain my own mental attitude and not to dispute with those who have found healing for themselves. Remedies vary according to the nature of the disease; those which benefit some may injure others.

PHILOSOPHY-How far it is open to censure or not-On what points its adherents may be considered believers or unbelievers, orthodox or heretical-What they have borrowed from the true doctrine to render their chimerical theories acceptable-Why the minds of men swerve from the truth-What criteria are available wherewith to separate the pure gold from the alloy in their systems.

I proceeded from the study of scholastic theology to that of philosophy. It was plain to me that, in order to discover where the professors of any branch of knowledge have erred, one must make a profound study of that science; must equal, may surpass, those who know most of it, so as to penetrate into secrets of it unknown to them. Only by this method can they be completely answered, and of this method I can find no trace in the theologians of Islam. In theological writings devoted to the refutation of philosophy I have only found a tangled mass of phrases full of contradictions and mistakes, and incapable of deceiving, I will not say a critical mind, but even the common crowd. Convinced that to dream of refuting a doctrine before having thoroughly comprehended it was like shooting at an object in the dark, I devoted myself zealously to the study of philosophy; but in books only and without the aid of a teacher. I gave up to this work all the leisure remaining from teaching and from composing work on law. There were then attending my lectures three hundred of the students of Baghdad. With the help of God, these studies, carried on in secret so to speak, put me in a condition to thoroughly comprehend philosophical systems within a space of two years. I then spent about a year in meditating on these systems after having thoroughly understood them. I turned them over and over in my mind till they were thoroughly clear of all obscurity. In this manner I acquired a complete knowledge of all their subterfuges and subtleties, of what was truth and what was illusion in them.

I now proceed to give a resume of these doctrines. I ascertained that they were divided into different varieties, and that their adherents might be ranged under diverse heads. All, in spite of their diversity, are marked with the stamp of infidelity and irreligion, although there is a considerable difference between the ancient and modern, between the first and last of these philosophers, according as they have missed or approximated to the truth in a greater or less degree.

Concerning the philosophical sects and the stigma of Infidelity which attaches to them all.

The philosophical systems, in spite of their number and variety, may be reduced to three: (1) The Materialists; (2) The Naturalists; (3) The Theists.

(1) The Materialists. They reject an intelli- gent and omnipotent Creator and Disposer of the Universe. In their view the world exists from all eternity and had no author. The animal comes from semen and semen from the animal; so, it has always been and will always be; those who maintain this doctrine are atheists.

(2) The Naturalists. These devote themselves to the study of nature and of the marvellous phenomena of the animal and vegetable world.

Having carefully analysed animal organs with the help of anatomy, struck with the wonders of God's work and with the wisdom therein revealed, they are forced to admit the existence of a wise Creator Who knows the end and purpose of everything. And certainly no one can study anatomy and the wonderful mechanism of living things without being obliged to confess the pro- found wisdom of Him Who has framed the bodies of animals and especially of man. But carried away by their natural research they believed that the existence of a being absolutely depended upon the proper equilibrium of its organism. According to them, as the latter perishes and is destroyed, so is the thinking faculty which is bound up with it; and as they assert that the restoration of a thing once destroyed to existence is unthinkable, they deny the immortality of the soul. Consequently, they deny heaven, hell, resurrection, and judgment. Acknowledging neither a recompense for good deeds nor a punishment or evil ones, they fling off all authority and plunge into sensual pleasures with the avidity of brutes. These also ought to be called atheists, for the true faith depends not only on the acknowledgement of God, but of His Apostle and of the Day of Judgment. And although they acknowledge God and His attributes, they deny a judgment to come.

(3) Next come the Theists. Among them should be reckoned Socrates, who was the teacher of Plato, as Plato was of Aristotle. This latter drew up for his disciples the rules of logic, organised the sciences, elucidated what was formerly obscure, and expounded what had not been understood. This school refuted the systems of the two others, i.e. the Materialists and Naturalists; but in exposing their mistaken and perverse beliefs, they made use of arguments which they should not. "God suffices to protect the faithful in war." (Koran, xxxiii, 25).

Aristotle also contended with success against the theories of Plato, Socrates, and the theists who had preceded him, and separated himself entirely from them; but he could not eliminate from his doctrine the stains of infidelity and heresy which disfigure the teaching of his predecessors. We should therefore consider them all as unbelievers, as well as the so-called Mussulman philosophers, such as Ibn Sina (Avicenna) and Farabi, who have adopted their systems.

Let us, however, acknowledge that among Mussulman philosophers none have better interpreted the doctrine of Aristotle than the latter. What others have handed down as his teaching is full of error, confusion, and obscurity adopted to disconcert the reader. The unintelligible can neither be accepted nor rejected. The philosophy of Aristotle, all serious knowledge of which we owe to the translation of these two learned men, may be divided into three portions; the first contains matter justly chargeable with impiety, the second is tainted with heresy, and the third we are obliged to reject absolutely. We proceed to details:

Divisions of the philosophic sciences

These sciences, in relation to the aim we have set before us, may be divided into six sections: (1) Mathematics; (2) Logic; (3) Physics; (4) Metaphysics; (5) Politics; (6) Moral Philosophy.

(1) *Mathematics* comprises the knowledge of calculation, geometry, and cosmography; it has no connection with the religious sciences, and proves nothing for or against religion; its rests on a foundation of proofs which, once known and understood, cannot be refuted. Mathematics tend, however, to produce two bad results.

The first is this: Whoever studies this science admires the subtlety and clearness of its proofs. His confidence in philosophy increases, and he thinks that all its departments are capable of the same clearness and solidity of proof as mathematics. But when he hears people speak of the unbelief and impiety of mathematicians, of their professed disregard for the Divine Law, which is notorious, it is true that, out of regard for authority, he echoes these accusations, but he says to himself at the same time that, if there was truth in religion, it would not have escaped those who have displayed so much keenness of intellect in the study of mathematics.

Next, when he becomes aware of the unbelief and rejection of religion on the part of these learned men, he concludes that to reject religion is reasonable. How many of such men gone astray I have met whose sole argument was that just mentioned. And supposing one puts to them the following objection: "It does not follow that a man who excels in one branch of knowledge excels in all others, nor that he should be equally versed in jurisprudence, theology, and medicine. It is possible to be entirely ignorant of metaphysics, and yet to be an excellent grammarian. There are past masters in every science who are entirely ignorant of other branches of knowledge. The arguments of the ancient philosophers are rigidly demonstrative in mathematics and only conjectural in religious questions. In order in ascertain this, one must proceed to a thorough examination of the matter." Supposing, I say, one makes the above objection to these "apes of unbelief," they find it distasteful. Falling a prey to their passions, to a besotted vanity, and the wish to pass for learned men, they persist in maintaining the pre-eminence of mathematicians in all branches of knowledge. This is a serious evil, and for this reason those who study mathematics should be checked from going too far in their research. For though far removed as it may be from the things of religion, this study, serving as it does as an introduction to the philosophic systems, casts over religion its malign influence. It is rarely that a man devotes himself to if without robbing himself of his faith and casting off the restraints of religion.

The second evil comes from the sincere but ignorant Mussulman who thinks the best way to defend religion is by rejecting all the exact sciences. Accusing their professors of being astray, he rejects their theories of the eclipses of the sun and moon, and condemns them in the name of religion. These accusations are carried far and wide, they reach the ears of the philosopher who knows that these theories rest on infallible proofs; far from losing confidence in them, he believes, on the contrary, that Islam has ignorance and the denial of scientific proofs for its basis, and his devotion to philosophy increases with his hatred to religion.

It is therefore a great injury to religion to suppose that the defence of Islam involves the condemnation of the exact sciences. The religious law contains nothing which approves them or condemns them, and in their turn, they make no attack on religion. The words of the Prophet, "The sun and the moon are two signs of the power of God; they are not eclipsed for the birth or the death of anyone; when you see these signs take refuge in prayer and invoke the name of God"-these words, I say, do not in any way condemn the astronomical calculations which define the orbits of these two bodies, their conjunction and opposition according to particular laws. But as for the so-called tradition, "When God reveals Himself in anything, He abases Himself thereto," it is unauthentic, and not found in any trustworthy collection of the traditions.

Such is the bearing and the possible danger of mathematics.

(2) *Logic.* This science, in the same manner, contains nothing for or against religion. Its object is the study of different kinds of proofs and syllogisms, the conditions which should hold between the premises of a proposition, the way to combine them, the rules of a good definition, and the art of formulating it. For knowledge consists of conceptions which spring from a definition or of convictions which arise from proofs. There is therefore nothing censurable in this science, and it is laid under contribution by theologians as well as by philosophers. The only difference is that the latter use a

particular set of technical formulae and that they push their divisions and subdivisions further.

It may be asked, what, then, this has to do with the grave questions of religion, and on what ground opposition should be offered to the methods of logic? The objector, it will be said, can only inspire the logician with an unfavourable opinion of the intelligence and faith of his adversary, since the latter's faith seems to be based upon such objections. But it must be admitted, logic is liable to abuse. Logicians demand in reasoning certain conditions which lead to absolute certainty, but when they touch on religious questions, they cannot longer postulate these conditions, and ought therefore to relax their habitual rigour. It happens, accordingly, that a student who is enamoured of the evidential methods of logic, hearing his teachers accused of irreligion, believes that this irreligion reposes on proofs as strong as those of logic, and immediately, without attempting the study of metaphysics, shares their mistake. This is a serious disadvantage arising from the study of logic.

(3) *Physics.* The object of this science is the study of the bodies which compose the universe: the sky and the stars, and, here below, simple elements such as air. earth, water. fire, and compound bodies-animals, plants and minerals; the reasons of their changes, developments, and intermixture. By the nature of its research, it is closely connected with the study of medicine, the object of which is the human body, its principal and secondary organs, and the law which governs their changes. Religion having no fault to find with medical science cannot justly do so with physical, except on some special matters which we have mentioned in the work

entitled The Destruction of the Philosophers. Besides these primary questions there are some subordinate ones depending on them, on which physical science is open to objection. But all physical science rests, as we believe, on the following principle: Nature is entirely subject to God; incapable of acting by itself, it is an instrument in the hand of the Creator; sun, moon, stars and elements are subject to God and can produce nothing of themselves. In a word, nothing in nature can act spontaneously and apart from God.

(4) *Metaphysics.* This is the fruitful breeding-ground of the errors of philosophers. Here they can no longer satisfy the laws of rigorous argumentation such as logic demands, and this is what explains the disputes which arise between them in the study of metaphysics. The system most closely akin to the system of the Muhammadan doctrines is that of Aristotle as expounded to us by Farabi and Avicenna. The sum total of their errors can be reduced to twenty propositions: three of them are irreligious, and the other seventeen here- tical. It was in order to combat their system that we wrote the work Destruction of the Philosophers. The three propositions in which they are opposed to all the doctrines of Islam are the following:

(1) Bodies do not rise again; spirits alone will be rewarded or punished; future punishments will be therefore spiritual and not physical. They are right in admitting spiritual punishments, for there will be such; but they are wrong in rejecting physical punishments, and contradicting in this manner the assertions of the Divine Law.

(2) "God takes cognizance of universals, not of specials." This is manifestly irreligious. The Koran asserts truly, "Not an atom's weight in heaven or earth can escape His knowledge" (x 62).

(3) They maintain that the universe exists from all eternity and will never end.

None of these propositions have ever been admitted by Moslems.

Besides this, they deny that God has attributes, and maintain that He knows by His essence only and not by means of any attribute accessory to His essence. In this point they approach the doctrine of the Mutazilites, doctrines which we are not obliged to condemn as irreligious. On the contrary, in our work entitled Criteria of the differences which divide Islam from Atheism, we have proved the wrongness of these who accuse of irreligion everything which is opposed to their way of looking at things.

(5) Political Science. The professors of this confine themselves to drawing up the rules which regulate temporal matters and the royal power. They have borrowed their theories on this point from the books which God has revealed to His prophets and from the sentences of ancient sages, gathered by tradition.

(6) *Moral Philosophy.* The professors of this occupy themselves with defining the attributes and qualities of the soul, grouping them according to genus and species, and pointing out the way to moderate and control them. They have borrowed this system from the Sufis. These devout men, who are always engaged in invoking the name of God, in

combating concupiscence and following the way of God by renouncing the pleasures of this world, have received, while in a state of ecstasy, revelations regarding the qualities of the soul, its defects and its evil inclinations. These revelations they have published, and the philosophers making use of them have introduced them into their own systems in order to embellish and give currency to their falsehoods. In the times of the philosophers, as at every other period, there existed some of these fervent mystics. God does not deprive this world of them, for they are its sustainers, and they draw down to it the blessings of heaven according to the tradition: "It is by them that you obtain rain, it is by them that you receive your subsistence." Such were "the Companions of the Cave," who lived in ancient times, as related by the Koran (xviii). Now this mixture of moral and philosophic doctrine with the words of the prophet and those of the Sufis gives rise to two dangers, one for the upholder of those doctrines, the other for their opponent.

The danger for their opponent is serious. A narrow-minded man, finding in their writings moral philosophy mixed with unsupported theories, believes that he ought to entirely reject them and to condemn those who profess them. Having only heard them from their mouth he does not hesitate in his ignorance to declare them false because those who teach them are in error. It is as if someone was to reject the profession of faith made by Christians. "There is only one God and Jesus is His prophet," simply because it proceeds from Christians and without inquiring whether it is the profession of this creed or the denial of Muhammad's prophetic mission which makes Christians infidels. Now if they are only infidels because of their rejection of our prophet, we are not entitled to reject those of their doctrines which do not wear the stamp of infidelity. In a word, truth does not cease to be true because it is found among them. Such, however, is the tendency of weak mind they judge the truth according to its professors instead of judging its professors by the standard of the truth. But a liberal spirit will take as its guide this maxim of the prince of believers, Ali the son of Abu Talib: "Do not seek for the truth by means of men; find first the truth and then you will recognise those who follow it." This is the procedure followed by a wise man. Once in possession of the truth he examines the basis of various doctrines which come before him, and when he has found them true, he accepts them without troubling himself whether the person who teaches them is sincere or a deceiver. Much rather, remembering how gold is buried in the bowels of the earth, the endeavours to disengage the truth from the mass of errors in which it is engulfed. The skilled coin-assayer plunges without hesitation his hand into the purse of the coiner of false money, and, relying on experience, separates good coins from bad. It is the ignorant rustic, and not the experienced assayer, who will ask why we should have anything to do with a false coiner. The unskilled swimmer must be kept away from the sea-shore, not the expert in diving. The child, not the charmer, must be forbidden to handle serpents.

As a matter of fact, men have such a good opinion of themselves, of their mental superiority and intellectual depth; they believe themselves so skilled in discerning the true from the false, the path of safety from those of error, that they should be forbidden as much as possible the perusal of philosophic writings, for though they sometimes escape the danger just pointed out, they cannot avoid that which we are about to indicate.

Some of the maxims found in my works regarding the mysteries of religion have met with objectors of an inferior rank in science, whose intellectual penetration is insufficient to fathom such depths. They assert that these maxims are borrowed from the ancient philosophers whereas the truth is that they are the fruit of my own meditations, but as the proverb says, 'Sandal follows the impress of sandal.'[1] Some of them are found in our books of religious law, but the greater part are derived from the writings of the Sufis.

But even if they were borrowed exclusively from the doctrines of the philosophers, is it right to reject an opinion when it is reasonable in itself, supported by solid proofs, and contradicting neither the Koran nor the traditions? If we adopt this method and reject every truth which has chanced to have been proclaimed by an impostor, how many truths we should have to reject! How many verses of the Koran and traditions of the prophets and Sufi discourses and maxims of sages we must close our ears to because the author of the Treatise of the Brothers of Purity has inserted them in his writings in order to further his cause, and in order to lead minds gradually astray in the paths of error! The consequence of this procedure would be that impostors would snatch truths out of our hands in order to embellish their own works. The wise man,

[1] i.e., There is nothing new under the sun.

at least, should not make common cause with the bigot blinded by ignorance.

Honey does not become impure because it may happen to have been placed in the glass which the surgeon uses for cupping purposes. The impurity of blood is due, not to its contact with this glass, but to a peculiarity inherent in its own nature; this peculiarity, not existing in honey, cannot be communicated to it by its being placed in the cupping glass; it is therefore wrong to regard it as impure. Such is, however, the whimsical way of looking at things found in nearly all men. Every word proceeding from an authority which they approve is accepted by them, even were it false; every word proceeding from one whom they suspect is rejected, even were it true. In every case they judge of the truth according to its professors and nor of men ac- cording to the truth which they profess, a *neplus ultra* of error. Such is the peril in which philosophy involves its opponents.

The second danger threatens those who accept the opinions of the philosophers. When, for instance, we read the treatises of the "Brothers of Purity" and other works of the same kind, we find in them sentences spoken by the Prophet and quotations from the Sufis. We approve these works; we give them our confidence; and we finish by accepting the errors which they contain, because of the good opinion of them with which they have inspired us at the outset. Thus, by insensible degrees, we are led astray. In view of this danger the reading of philosophic writings so full of vain and delusive utopias should be for- bidden, just as the slippery banks of a river are forbidden to one who knows not how to swim. The perusal of these false teachings must be prevented just as one prevents children from touching serpents. A snake-charmer himself will abstain from touching snakes in the presence of his young child, because he knows that the child, believing himself as clever as his father, will not fail to imitate him; and in order to lend more weight to his prohibition the charmer will not touch a serpent under the eyes of his son.

Such should be the conduct of a learned man who is also wise. But the snake-charmer, after having taken the serpent and separated the venom from the antidote, having put the letter on one side and destroyed the venom, ought not to withhold the antidote from those who need it. In the same way the skilled coin-assayer, after having punishment in the bag of the false corner, taken out the good coins and thrown away the bad ones, ought not to refuse the good to those who need and ask for it. Such should be the conduct of the learned man. If the patient feels a certain dislike of the antidote because he knows that it is taken from a snake whose body is the receptacle of poison, he should be disabused of his fallacy. If a beggar hesitates to take a piece of gold which he knows comes from the purse of a false coiner, he should be told that his hesitation is a pure mistake which would deprive him of the advantage which he seeks. It should be proved to him that the contact of the good coins with the bad does not injure the former and does not improve the latter. In the same way the contact of truth with falsehood does not change truth unto falsehood, any more than it changes falsehood into truth.

Thus much, then, we have to say regarding the inconvenience and dangers which spring from the study of philosophy.

Sufism

When I had finished my examination of these doctrines, I applied myself to the study of Sufism. I saw that in order to understand it thoroughly one must combine theory with practice. The aim which the Sufis set before them is as follows: To free the soul from the tyrannical yoke of the passions, to deliver it from its wrong inclinations and evil instincts, in order that in the purified heart there should only remain room for God and for the invocation of His holy name.

As it was more easy to learn their doctrine than to practise it, I studied first of all those of their books which contain it: The Nourishment of Hearts, by Abu Talib of Mecca, the works of Harethel Muhasibi, and the fragments which still remain of Junaid, Shibli, Abu Yezid Bustami and other leaders (whose souls may God sanctify). I acquired a thorough knowledge of their research- es, and I learned all that was possible to learn of their methods by study and oral teaching. It became clear to me that the last stage could not be reached by mere instruction, but only by transport, ecstasy, and the transformation of the moral being.

To define health and satiety, to penetrate their causes and conditions, is quite another thing from being well and satisfied. To define drunken- ness, to know that it is caused by vapours which rise from the stomach and cloud the seat of intelligence, is quite a different thing to being drunk. The drunken man has no idea of the nature of drunkenness, just because he is drunk and not in a condition to understand anything, while the doctor, not being under the influence of drunkenness, knows its character and laws. Or if the doctor falls ill, he has a theoretical knowledge of the health of which he is deprived.

In the same way there is a considerable difference between knowing renouncement, comprehending its conditions and causes, and practising renouncement and detachment from the things of this world. I saw that Sufism consists in experiences rather than in definitions, and that what I was lacking belonged to the domain, not of instruction, but of ecstasy and intuition.

The researches to which I had devoted myself, the path which I had traversed in studying religious and speculative branches of knowledge, had given me a firm faith in three things-God, Inspiration, and the Last Judgment. These three fundamental articles of belief were confirmed in me, not merely by definite arguments, but by a chain of causes circumstances, and proofs which it is impossible to recount. I saw that one can only hope for salvation by devotion and the conquest of one's passions, a procedure which presupposes renouncement and detachment from this world or falsehood in order to turn towards eternity and meditation on God. Finally, I saw that the only condition of success was to sacrifice honours and riches and to sever the ties and attachments of worldly life.

Coming seriously to consider my state, I found myself bound down on all sides by these trammels. Examining my actions, the most fair- seeming of which were my lecturing and professorial occupations, I found to my surprise that I was engrossed in several studies of little value, and profitless as regards my salvation. I probed the motives of my teaching and found that, in place of being sincerely consecrated to God, it was only actuated by a vain desire of honour and reputation. I perceived that I was on the edge of an abyss, and that without an immediate conversion I should be doomed to eternal fire. In these reflections I spent a long time. Still a prey to uncertainty, one day I decided to leave Baghdad and to give up everything; the next day I gave up my resolution. I advanced one step and immediately relapsed. In the morning I was sincerely resolved only to occupy myself with the future life; in the evening a crowd of carnal thoughts assailed and dispersed my resolutions. On the one side the world kept me bound to my post in the chairs of covetousness, on the other side the voice of religion cried to me, "Up! Up! thy life is nearing its end, and thou hast a long journey to make. All the pretended knowledge is nought but falsehood and fantasy. If thou dost not think now of thy salvation, when wilt thou think of it? If thou dost not break the chains to-day, when will thou break them?" Then my resolve was strengthened, I wished to give up all and flee; but the Tempter, returning to the attack, said, "You are suffering from a transitory feeling; don't give way to it, for it will soon pass. If you obey it, if you give up this fine position, this honourable post exempt from trouble and rivalry, this seat of authority safe from attack, you will regret it later on without being able to recover it."

Thus, I remained, torn-asunder by the opposite forces of earthly passions and religious aspirations, for about six months from the month Rajab of the year A.D. 1096. At the close of them my will yielded, and I gave myself up to destiny. God caused an impediment, to chain my tongue and prevented me from lecturing. Vainly I desired, in the interest of my pupils, to go on with my teaching, but my mouth became dumb. The silence to which I was condemned cast me into a violent despair; my stomach became weak; I lost all appetite; I could neither swallow a morsel of bread nor drink a drop of water.

The enfeeblement of my physical powers was such that the doctors, despairing of saving me, said, "The mischief is in the heart, and had communicated itself to the whole organism; there is no hope unless the cause of his grievous sadness be arrested."

Finally, conscious of my weakness and the prostration of my soul, I took refuge in God as a man at the end of himself and without resources. "He who hears the wretched when they cry" (Koran, xxvii. 63) deigned to hear me; He made easy to me the sacrifice of honours, wealth, and family. I gave out publicly that I intended to make the pilgrimage to Mecca, while I secretly resolved to go to Syria, not wishing that the Caliph (may God magnify him) or my friends should know my intention of settling in that country. I made all kinds of clever excuses for leaving Bagdad with the fixed intention of not returning thither. The Imams of irak criticised me with one accord. Not one of them could admit that this sacrifice had a religious motive, because they considered my position as the highest attainable in the religious community. "Behold how far their knowledge goes!" (Koran, liii 31). All kinds of explanations of my conduct were forthcoming. Those who were outside the limits of Irak attributed it to the fear with which the Government inspired me. Those who were on the spot and saw how the authorities wished to detain me, their displeasure at my resolution and my refusal of their request, said to them- selves, "It is a calamity which one can only impute to a fate which has befallen the Faithful and Learning!"

At last, I left Bagdad, giving up all my fortune. Only, as lands and property in Irak can afford an endowment for pious purposes, I obtained a legal authorisation to preserve as much as was necessary for my support and that of my children; for there is surely nothing more lawful in the world than that a learned man should provide sufficient to support his family. I then betook myself to Syria, where I remained for two years, which I devoted to retirement, meditation, and devout exercises. I only thought of self- improvement and discipline and of purification of the heart by prayer in going through the forms of devotion which the Sufis had taught me. I used to live a solitary life in the Mosque of Damascus and was in the habit of spending my days on the minaret after closing the door behind him.

From thence I proceeded to Jerusalem, and every day secluded myself in the Sanctuary of the Rock.[2] After that I felt a desire to accomplish the Pilgrimage, and to receive a full effusion of grace by visiting Mecca, Medina, and the Tomb of the Prophet. After visiting the shrine of the Friend of God (Abraham), I went to the Hedjaz. Finally, the longings of my heart and the prayers of my children brought me back to my country although I was so firmly resolved at first never to revisit it. At any rate I meant, if I did return, to live there solitary and in religious meditation; but events, family cares and vicissitudes of little changed my resolutions and troubled my meditative calm. However irregular the intervals which I could give to devotional ecstasy, my confidence in it did not diminish; and the more I was diverted by hindrances, the more steadfastly I returned to it.

---

[2] In the Mosque of Omar.

Ten years passed in this manner. During my successive periods of meditation there were revealed to me things impossible to recount. All that I shall say for the edification of the reader is this I learnt from a sure source that the Sufis are the true pioneers on the path of God: that there is nothing more beautiful than their life, nor more praiseworthy than their rule of conduct, nor purer than their morality. The intelligence of thinkers, the wisdom of philosophers, the knowledge of the most learned doctors of the law would in vain combine their efforts in order to modify or improve their doctrine and morals; it would be impossible. With the Sufis, repose and movement, exterior, or interior, are illumined with the light which proceeds from the Central Radiance of Inspiration. And what other light could shine on the face of the earth? In a word, what can one criticise in them? To purge the heart of all that does not belong to God is the first step in their cathartic method. The drawing up of the heart by prayer is the keystone of it, as the cry "Allahu Akbar" (God is great) is the keystone of prayer, and the last stage is the being lost in God. I say the last stage, with reference to what may be reached by an effort of will; but, to tell the truth, it is only the first stage in the life of contemplation, the vestibule by which the initiated enter.

From the time that they set out on this path, revelations commence for them. They come to see in the waking state angels and souls of prophets; they hear their voices and wise counsels. By means of this contemplation of heavenly forms and images they rise by degrees to heights which human language cannot reach, which one cannot even indicate without falling into great and inevitable errors. The degree of proximity to Deity which they attain is regarded by some as intermixture of being (haloul), by others as identification (ittihad), by others as intimate union (wasl). But all these expressions are wrong, as we have explained in our work entitled, The Chief Aim. Those who have reached that stage should confine themselves to repeating the verse-

> What I experience I shall not try to say:
>
> Call me happy, but ask me no more,

In short, he who does not arrive at the intuition of these truths by means of ecstasy, knows only the name of inspiration. The minerals wrought by the saints are, in fact, merely the earliest forms of prophetic manifestation. Such was the state of the Apostle of God when, before receiving his commission, he retired to Mount Hira to give himself up to such intensity of prayer and meditation that the Arabs said: Muhammad is become enamoured of God."

This state, then, can be revealed to the initiated in ecstasy, and to him who is incapable of ecstasy, by obedience and attention, on condition that he frequents the society of Sufis till he arrives, so to speak, at an imitative initiation. Such is the faith which one can obtain by remaining among them, and intercourse with them is never painful.

But even when we are deprived of the ad- vantage of their society, we can comprehend the possibility of this state (revelation by means of ecstasy) by a chain of manifest proofs. We have explained this in the treatise entitled Marvels of the Heart, which forms part of our work, The Revival of the Religious Science. The certitude derived from proofs is called "knowledge"; passing into the state we describe is called "transport"; believing the experience of others and oral transmission is "faith." Such are the three degrees of knowledge, as it is written, "The Lord will raise to different ranks those among you who have believed and those who have received knowledge from Him," (Koran, lviii. 12).

But behind those who believe comes a crowd of ignorant people who deny the reality of Sufism, hear discourses on it with incredulous irony, and treat as charlatans those who profess it. To this ignorant crowd the verse applies: "There are those among them who come to listen to thee, and when they leave thee, ask of those who have received knowledge, 'What has he just said?" There are they whose hearts God has sealed up with blindness and who only follow their passions".

Among the number of convictions which I owe to the practice of the Sufi rule is the know- ledge of the true nature of inspiration. This knowledge is of such great importance that I proceed to expound it in detail.

The reality of inspiration: Its importance for the human race

The substance of man at the moment of its creation is a simple monad, devoid of knowledge of the worlds subject to the Creator, worlds whose infinite number is only known to Him, as the Koran says: "Only thy Lord knoweth the number of His armies."

Man arrives at this knowledge by the aid of his perceptions; each of his senses is given him that he may comprehend the world of created things, and by the term "world" we understand the different species of creatures. The first sense revealed to man is touch, by means of which he perceives a certain group of qualities-heat, cold, moist, dry. The sense of touch does not perceive colours and forms, which are for it as though they did not exist. Next comes the sense of sight, which makes him acquainted with colours and forms; that is to say, with that which occupies the highest rank in the world of sensation. The sense of hearing succeeds, and then the senses of smell and taste.

When the human being can elevate himself above the world of sense, towards the age of seven, he receives the faculty of discrimination; he enters then upon a new phase of existence and can experience, thanks to this faculty, impressions, superior to those of the senses, which do not occur in the sphere of sensation.

He then passes to another phase and receives reason, by which he discerns things necessary, possible, and impossible; in a word, all the notions which he could not combine in the former stages of his existence. But beyond reason and at a higher level a new faculty of vision is bestowed upon him, by which he perceives invisible things, the secrets of the future and other concepts as inaccessible to reason as the concepts of reason are inaccessible to mere discrimination and what is perceived by discrimination to the senses. Just as the man possessed only of discrimination rejects and denies the notions acquired by reason, so do certain rationalists reject and deny the notion of inspiration. It is a proof of their profound ignorance; for, instead of argument, they merely deny inspiration as a sphere unknown and possessing no real existence. In the same way, a man blind from birth, who knows neither by experience nor by information what colours and forms are, neither knows nor understands them when someone speaks of them to him for the first time.

God, wishing to render intelligible to men the idea of inspiration, has given them a kind of glimpse of it in sleep. In fact, man perceives while asleep the things of the invisible world either clearly manifest or under the veil of allegory to be subsequently lifted by divination. If, however, one was to say to a person who had never himself experienced these dreams that, in a state of lethargy resembling death and during the complete suspension of sight, hearing, and all the senses, a man can see the things of the invisible world, this person would exclaim, and seek to prove the impossibility of these visions by some such argument as the following: "The sensitive faculties are the causes of perception. Now, if one can perceive certain things when one is in full possession of these faculties, how much more is their perception impossible when these faculties are suspended."

The falsity of such an argument is shown by evidence and experience. For in the same way as reason constitutes a particular phase of existence in which intellectual concepts are perceived which are hidden from the senses, similarly, inspiration is a special state in which the inner eye discovers, revealed by a celestial light, mysteries out of the reach of reason. The doubts which are raised regarding inspiration relate (1) to its possibility, (2) to its real and actual existence, (3) to its manifestation in this or that person.

To prove the possibility of inspiration is to prove that it belongs to a category of branches of knowledge which cannot be attained by reason. It is the same with medical science and astronomy. He who studies them is obliged to recognise that they are derived solely from the revelation and special grace of God. Some astronomical phenomena only occur once in a thousand years; how then can we know them by experience?

We may say the same of inspiration, which is one of the branches of intuition knowledge. Further, the perception of things which are beyond the attainment of reason is only one of the features peculiar to inspiration, which possesses a great number of others. The characteristic which we have mentioned is only, as it were, a drop of water in the ocean, and we have mentioned it because people experience what is analogous to it in dreams and in the sciences of medicine and astronomy. These branches of knowledge belong to the domain of prophetic miracles, and reason cannot attain to them.

As to the other characteristic of inspiration they are only revealed to adepts in Sufism and in a state of ecstatic transport. The little that we know of the nature of inspiration we owe to the kind of likeness to it which we find in sleep; without that we should be incapable of comprehending it, and consequently of believing in it, for conviction results from comprehension. The process of initiation into Sufism exhibits this likeness to inspiration from the first. There is in it a kind of ecstasy proportioned to the condition of the person initiated, and a degree of certitude and conviction which cannot be attained by reason. This single fact is sufficient to make us believe in inspiration.

We now come to deal with doubts relative to the inspiration of a particular prophet. We shall not arrive at certitude on this point except by ascertaining, either by ocular evidence or by reliable tradition, the facts relating to that prophet. When we have ascertained the real nature of inspiration and proceed to the serious study of the Koran and the traditions, we shall then know certainly that Muhammed is the greatest of prophets. After that we should fortify you conviction by verifying the truth of his preaching and the salutary effect which it has upon the soul. We should verify in experience the truth of sentences such as the following: "He who makes his con- duct accord with his knowledge receives from God more knowledge"; or this, "God delivers to the oppressor him who favours injustice"; or again, "Whosoever when rising in the morning has only one anxiety (to please God), God will preserve him from all anxiety in this world and the next."

When we have verified these sayings in experience thousands of times, shall be in possession of a certitude on which doubt can obtain no hold. Such is the path we must traverse in order to realise the truth of inspiration. It is not a question of finding out whether a rod has been changed into a serpent, or whether the moon has been split in two[3] If we regard miracles in isolation, without their countless attendant circumstances, we shall be liable to confound them with magic and falsehood, or to regard them as a means of leading menastry, as it is written, "God misleads and directs as He. chooses" (Koran, xxxv. 9); we shall find ourselves involved in all the difficulties which the question of miracles raises. If, for instance, we believe that eloquence of style is a proof of inspiration, it is possible that an eloquent style composed with this object may inspire us with a false belief in the inspiration him who wields it. The supernatural should be only one of the constituents which go to from our belief, without our placing too much reliance on this or that detail. We should rather resemble a person who, learning a fact from a group of people, cannot point to this or that particular man as his informant, and who, not distinguishing between them, cannot explain precisely how his conviction regarding the fact has been formed.

Such are the characteristics of scientific certitude. As to the transport which permits men to see the truth and, so to speak, to handle it, it is only known to the Sufis. What I have just said regarding the true nature of inspiration is sufficient for the aim which I have proposed to myself. I may return to the subject later, if necessary.

I pass now to the causes of the decay of faith and show the means of bringing back those who have erred and of preserving them from the dangers which threaten them. To those who doubt

---

[3] A miracle ascribed to Muhammad.

because they are tinctured with the doctrine of the Ta'limites, my treatise entitled The Just Balance affords a sufficient guide; therefore, it is unnecessary to return to the subject here.

As to the vain theories of the Ibadat, I have grouped them in seven classes, and explained them in the work entitle Alchemy of Happiness. For those whose faith has been undermined by philosophy, so far that they deny the reality of inspiration, we have proved the truth and necessity of it, seeking our proofs in the hidden properties of medicines and of the heavenly bodies. It is for them that we have written this treatise, and the reason for our seeking for proofs in the sciences of medicine and of astronomy is because these sciences belong to the domain of philosophy. All those branches of knowledge which our opponents boast of astronomy medicine, physics, and divination-provide us with arguments in favour of the Prophet.

As to those who, professing a lip-faith in the Prophet, adulterate religion with philosophy, they really deny inspiration, since in their view the Prophet is only a sage whom a superior destiny has appointed as guide to men, and this view belies the true nature of inspiration. To believe in the Prophet is to admit that there is above intelligence a sphere in which are revealed to the inner vision truths beyond the grasp of intelligence, just as things seen are not apprehended by the sense of hearing, nor things understood by that of touch. If our opponent denies the existence of such a higher region, we can prove to him, not only its possibility, but its actuality. If, on the contrary, he admits its existence, he recognises at the same time that there are in that sphere things which reason cannot group; nay, which reason rejects as false and absurd. Suppose, for instance, that the fact of dreams occurring in sleep were not so common and notorious as it is, our wise men would not fail to repudiate the assertion that the secrets of the invisible world can be revealed while the senses are, so to speak, suspended.

Again, if it were to be said to one of them, "Is it possible that there is in the world a thing as small as a grain, which being carried into a city can destroy it and afterwards destroy itself so that nothing remains either of the city or of itself?" "Certainly," he would exclaim, "it is impossible and ridiculous." Such, however, is the effect of fire, which would certainly be disputed by one who had not witnessed it with his own eyes. Now, the refusal to believe in the mysteries of the other life is of the same kind.

As to the fourth cause of the spread of unbelief the decay of faith owing to the bad example set by learned men- there are three ways of checking it.

(1) One can answer thus: "The learned man whom you accuse of disobeying the divine law knows that he disobeys, as you do when you drink wine or exact usury or allow yourself in evil- speaking, lying, and slander. You know your sin and yield to it, not through ignorance, but because you are mastered by concupiscence. The same is the case with the learned man. How many believe in doctors who do not abstain from fruit and cold water when strictly forbidden them by a doctor! That does not prove that those things are not dangerous, or that their faith in the doctor was not solidly established. Similar errors of the part of learned men are to be imputed solely to their weakness."

(2) Or again one may say to a simple and ignorant man: "The learned man reckons upon his knowledge as a viaticum for the next life. He believes that his knowledge will save him and plead in his favour, and that his intellectual superiority will entitle him to indulgence; lastly, that if his knowledge increases his responsibility, it may also entitle him to a higher degree of consideration. All that is possible; and even if the learned man has neglected practice, he can at any rate produce proofs of his knowledge. But you, poor, witless one, if, like him, you neglect practice, destitute as you are of knowledge, you will perish without anything to plead in your favour."

(3) Or one may answer, and this reason is the true one: "The truly learned man only sins through carelessness, and does not remain in a state of impenitence. For real knowledge shows sin to be a deadly poison, and the other world to be superior to this. Convinced of this truth, man ought not to exchange the precious for the vile. But the knowledge of which we speak is not derived from sources accessible to human diligence, and that is why progress in mere worldly knowledge renders the sinner more hardened in his revolt against God.

True knowledge, on the contrary, inspires in him who is initiate in it more fear and more reverence, and raises a barrier of defence between him and sin. He may slip and stumble, it is true, as is inevitable with one encompassed by human infirmity, but these slips and stumbles will not weaken his faith. The true Moslem succumbs occasionally to temptation, but he repents and will not persevere obstinately in the path of error.

I pray God the Omnipotent to place us in the ranks of His chosen, among the number of those whom He directs in the path of safety, in whom He inspires fervour lest they forget Him; whom He cleanses from all defilement, that nothing may remain in them except Himself; yea, of those whom He indwells completely, that they may adore none beside Him.

www.ingramcontent.com/pod-product-compliance
Ingram Content Group UK Ltd.
Pitfield, Milton Keynes, MK11 3LW, UK
UKHW021410190726
13845UKWH00028B/1004

9 789394 770959